Executive Functioning Workbook

By

MELISSA MULLIN, PH.D. AND KAREN FRIED, PSY.D.

TARGETED LEARNING CONCEPTS™

ABOUT THE AUTHORS

Karen Fried, Psy.D., and Melissa Mullin, Ph.D., are the owners and Directors of the K&M Center. As creators of the K&M Center, Karen and Melissa set themselves a mission to help every student learn to his or her potential. Melissa and Karen work with parents, teachers, tutors and other professionals to individualize a truly effective program for each child. The joy of helping children do well in school, and in life, motivates Melissa and Karen to provide the best learning center possible. After over 18 years of experience helping thousands of children learn to read, write and achieve in school, Karen and Melissa are now using their knowledge to create products that can guide teachers and parents who wish to help children learn.

KAREN FRIED holds a doctorate in psychology from Ryokan College. She received master's degrees both in Human Development and in Clinical Psychology, as well as a Certificate in Educational Therapy, from the College for Developmental Studies. A licensed MFT, she has practiced educational therapy and psychotherapy for over 15 years. Karen focused on learning disabilities and psychology in her graduate work to gain expertise in both the educational and emotional experiences of children. A founding board member of the Violet Solomon Oaklander Foundation, she conducts training for child therapists from the US and other countries. Karen is also on the Advisory Board of 826 LA.

MELISSA MULLIN fell in love with teaching while designing educational computer games for The Walt Disney Educational Media Company. She pursued her interest with enthusiasm, earning her Ph.D. in Educational Psychology, with a specialization in Learning and Instruction from UCLA. Upon receiving her doctorate Melissa began to specialize in helping children with learning differences. In her blog, www.bitsofwisdomforall.com, Melissa shares the insights about academic learning and life skills she gathers as she works with students and their families. In addition to teaching and creating educational products, Melissa enjoys spending time with her family, reading, hiking and skiing.

Learn more about Karen and Melissa and the products they have created at
www.kandmcenter.com

SPECIAL APPRECIATION TO OUR STAFF IN HELPING US DEVELOP AND TEST THESE MATERIALS:

EMMA PARSONS

JESSICA TRUGLIO

DESIGNED BY:

MEREDITH NOEL

ILLUSTRATIONS BY:

JOSEPH YUSS SIMON

THINKWELLSTUDIOS@ME.COM

EXECUTIVE FUNCTION WORKBOOK
TABLE OF CONTENTS

WHY LEARN EXECUTIVE FUNCTIONING SKILLS?

GOAL

The goal of this Workbook is to teach you how to build Executive Functioning skills and take control of your schoolwork. This program can help you develop the skills needed to become a better thinker and learner, but first, you have to understand how the brain works.

WHAT IS EXECUTIVE FUNCTIONING?

Executive Functioning--the manager part of the brain--is the "boss" that plans, starts, oversees, and finishes all kinds of tasks. Its powers, housed in the brain's frontal lobes, include:

INITIATION	• starting work
INHIBITION	• stopping off-task behavior
SHIFT	• moving from one activity to another
WORKING MEMORY	• remembering information for immediate use
PLANNING	• setting goals and the steps to accomplish them
ORGANIZING MATERIALS	• tracking items in work spaces
TIME MANAGEMENT	• allotting appropriate time for each task
MONITORING	• judging the quality and pace of work
EMOTIONAL CONTROL	• regulating stress and distractibility

RATIONALE

Brains are very complex and do many different jobs throughout the day. One important job that your brain has is to take in lots of information and then store it away in order for you to remember it later. The more efficiently you store the information in your brain, the easier it is to get it out again when you need it.

RESULTS

This Workbook is going to specifically work on the Executive Functioning part of the brain. Executive Functioning is the manager part of your brain that helps plan, organize and start tasks, set priorities, and pace activities. It helps you move from one subject to another, manage your stress, and finish what you started.

Since schoolwork involves a lot of tasks, the better Executive Functioning skills you have, the better you can do in school.

GAME PLAN

One of the most important parts of Executive Functioning is something called **metacognition**. Put simply, this means "thinking about thinking." In order to be a successful student, you need to know your own strengths and weaknesses and understand how you think and learn. By building metacognition, we are able to ask ourselves questions about what we need to do, set a goal, and then follow the steps needed to achieve our goal.

WHAT DOES THE PROGRAM DO?

The K&M Executive Functioning Program increases the student's ability to plan, start, and finish work autonomously. It **exercises the neurological activity that creates Executive Functioning** by identifying the student's aims and challenges, building thinking skills, and practicing organizational strategies. **The program establishes academic independence as the student determines goals and develops the habits that will achieve them.**

WHAT IS IN THE PROGRAM ?

- Self-assessment in each school subject
- Setting academic and personal goals
- Equipping a study space at home
- Organizing a backpack
- Using a planner to track daily, weekly, and long-term assignments
- Accurately estimating how long homework will take
- Scheduling time for homework, study, and other activities
- Breaking down long-term projects into daily tasks
- Active reading and study skills
- Taking useful notes on lectures and texts
- Test preparation and test-taking strategies
- Tracking progress and setting new goals

HOW DOES THE PROGRAM WORK?

The program increases the student's self-awareness of learning style, and active engagement in learning. To do so it follows **4 basic steps:**

- Assessment
- Setting goals
- Learning and practicing skills
- Tracking progress

The first step explores the student's own view of his or her challenges and strengths, and compares it to the parent's and teacher's **assessments**. The student can then better define his or her **goals**. Using games, the instructor shows how developing Executive Functioning skills will help the student attain those aims.

Schoolwork then serves to sharpen these abilities:

- Judging time accurately
- Building Working Memory
- Breaking down complex projects into manageable, orderly tasks
- Correctly estimating how long tasks will take
- Starting, stopping, and changing activities

At this point the instructor's **focused exercises and task-specific checklists make** long-term planning, active reading techniques, note-taking, test preparation, and test-taking strategies into solid habits. At every new step, **the student assesses his or her progress and creates new goals**.

EXECUTIVE FUNCTIONING refers to the manager part of your brain—the "boss" that plans, organizes, starts and finishes your tasks. Good executive functioning skills let you set priorities in your work, pace yourself while you work, handle work stress, go from one task to another, and complete what you started. The exercises in this workbook will strengthen your executive functioning skills.

Since schoolwork involves a lot of tasks, the better executive functioning skills you have, the better you can do in school. Would you like to know how you can improve your executive functioning skills?

Now it's time to take the EXECUTIVE FUNCTIONING QUESTIONNAIRE to see which executive functioning tasks you already do well and which ones you can strengthen to help you in school.

You will take the online questionnaire by clicking here:
http://www.kandmcenter.com/questionaire/SurveyTest01-05.htm

Now that the questionnaire is scored, record your scores here so that will have a reference to look back to as you work on the program.

EXECUTIVE FUNCTIONING QUESTIONNAIRE

		TOTAL
Group One: WORKING MEMORY		
Group Two: ORGANIZING MATERIALS		
Group Three: PLANNING TASKS		
Group Four: EMOTIONAL CONTROL		
Group Five: INITIATING WORK		
Group Six: INHIBITING BEHAVIOR		
Group Seven: MONITORING		
Group Eight: SHIFTING TO NEW TASKS		

How did you score in each area? Each of these 8 areas is an important piece of Executive Functioning. We might be successful in some areas but need to work at building others.

Are some areas higher and some areas lower? High scores may indicate your STRENGTHS in Executive Functioning. Low scores may indicate areas that you want to IMPROVE upon.

Here is a description of each area – see if you agree with your strengths and weaknesses…

<u>WORKING MEMORY</u>:

THE ABILITY TO REMEMBER INFORMATION FOR IMMEDIATE USE.

If you had a low score in this area, you may find it difficult to remember a series of directions or have a hard time with math problems that involve more than one step.

<u>ORGANIZING MATERIALS</u>:

THE ABILITY TO ORGANIZE OBJECTS IN WORK, PLAY, AND STORAGE AREAS.

Scoring low in this area may mean that you have a hard time keeping your binder organized or have difficulty keeping your books and backpack in order.

<u>PLANNING TASKS</u>:

THE ABILITY TO MANAGE TASKS BY SETTING GOALS AND DEVELOPING STEPS TO ACHIEVE THE GOALS.

If you scored low in this area, it may mean that you have a hard time figuring out what you need to do in order to finish a large project. You may read the assignment for your research paper over and over but not know what steps you need to complete in order to finish it on time.

<u>EMOTIONAL CONTROL</u>:

THE ABILITY TO REGULATE EMOTIONAL RESPONSES TO STRESS.

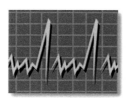

If this was a low area for you, you may have trouble getting over a poor grade on an assignment or find that you get frustrated often, which can get in the way of your school work.

<u>INITIATING WORK</u>:

THE ABILITY TO GET STARTED ON TASKS WITHOUT MANY PROMPTS AND CUES.

If you have trouble initiating work, this means you might have trouble finding the motivation to get started. Even if you know what you need to do, you keep wanting to put it off a little longer, until you realize that the deadline is coming up and you haven't gotten started yet.

INHIBITING BEHAVIOR:

THE ABILITY TO STOP ONE'S OWN BEHAVIOR AT AN APPROPRIATE TIME.

If you scored low in this area, you may find that it's hard for you to stop doing something, even if you know that you shouldn't be doing it. For example, you may know that you are not supposed to blurt out in class, but when your teacher isn't calling on you, you decide to say the answer anyway.

MONITORING:

THE ABILITY TO JUDGE THE QUANTITY AND QUALITY OF ONE'S WORK BASED ON EXPECTED STANDARDS.

If you have difficulty monitoring yourself, you might not have any idea how you got a low grade on an assignment that you thought you did well on. You may forget to go back and check your work when you're finished or not realize that you didn't follow the directions correctly.

SHIFTING TO NEW TASKS:

THE ABILITY TO TRANSITION FROM ONE ACTIVITY TO ANOTHER.

If you have trouble shifting to new tasks, it may be hard for you when the teacher asks you to put away an assignment that you are in the middle of. You want to finish it and have a difficult time starting the next assignment.

IT IS A GOOD IDEA TO HAVE YOUR PARENTS TAKE THE QUESTIONNAIRE AS WELL. SHARE THE INFORMATION YOU READ ABOVE WITH THEM AND SEE IF THEY AGREE WITH THEIR SCORES.

GOAL SETTING

Now that you've taken the questionnaire and done some self-reflection, it's time to set some goals for yourself. Keeping in mind your strengths and weaknesses and your answers to the questions above, what do you think are the top three things you'd like to improve in? Remember to make them reasonable – you don't want to set a goal that is impossible to reach.

For example, if you have trouble keeping your binder organized, a goal might be:

> "I will plan 10 minutes every night to clean out loose papers in my binder and file papers that I put in the front pocket."

MY GOALS:

1.

2.

3.

TIME TO REFLECT

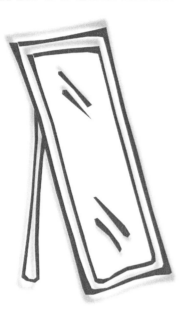

- What will my life look like when I achieve my goals?

- What do I need to do to make my life easier right now? Did I write a goal about this?

- What is going to motivate me to make these changes?

- Can I measure my progress with these goals? (If not, then you may want to rewrite them.)

For example, it's hard to measure "I will do my homework." But if you rewrite your goal as "I will use the Daily Homework Checklist each night to plan out my homework and check it off when I'm finished," then you can measure your progress over time.

HOW DO YOU SET UP A SUCCESSFUL EXECUTIVE FUNCTIONING PLAN?

• First, create a motivational plan for your student. Figure out something that will make him/her want to complete the checklist that you are going to give him/her. Make sure it is something that you can give to him/her every week if he/she completes the checklists.

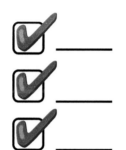

• Once you have the reward system that you and your student are happy with, you can present and review the checklist you want him/her to focus on. This program has many checklists provided for you. Pick the most important area you want your student to focus on and begin with that checklist.

• The most important part of the system is that the checklist needs to be signed daily.

The reward you have agreed upon is given for completing the checklists on a weekly basis. It is important to figure out what percent of the time your student is completing these tasks now. If your child is currently completing tasks 50% of the time, make the goal that he/she completes the task 80% of the time to receive the award. You want to set up the system to succeed, so don't set an unrealistic goal. You want to help your child earn the reward.

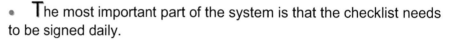

THIS IS IMPORTANT. Set your child up for success by implementing a program that is broken down into steps that are achievable. So, pick one thing that you think your child can do and set that as the first goal. For many of our students, the first goal is just to get the checklist signed.

If the goal is just to have the checklist signed daily, it means the student doesn't have to have everything in the backpack before they take it to get it signed. The parent and the teacher should reward the child for consistently presenting the checklist for their signature. Then the parent and the teacher can GENTLY remind the student to either write down assignments that are missing from the worksheet, turn in assignments that are missing, or add any materials to the backpack that should be there and aren't. Once the first goal is achieved consistently you can set the next goal.

Children with executive functioning difficulties need to have tasks broken down into manageable parts. That is the goal for parents and teachers to set for students in order to help these children achieve. Generally, students that are not organized tend to become overwhelmed by the prospect of the task ahead. This overwhelmed feeling is what stops them from being able to begin the task. By teaching students how to look at a task and mentally, or physically by making a list, break it down into manageable steps, you are teaching your child executive functioning skills.

The most important message is that children cannot do this alone. Building executive functioning skills need to start with an external structure guided by a coach, who can be a parent or a professional, who helps the student consistently review the steps needed to follow them, until the external structure becomes an internal monologue. This internal monologue is metacognition in action. Helping children learn the mantra "STOP, THINK, PLAN, DO, CHECK" is a good first step. Often the first step is the most difficult. Most children with executive functioning issues go straight to "DO" without taking time to do the other steps. So, if you can help your child STOP, THINK, PLAN and DO you will be instilling great executive functioning skills which will help your student in school and in life.

HERE IS WHAT TO THINK ABOUT BEFORE STARTING A NEW TASK:

1. STOP

- Stop what I am doing.

2. THINK

- What do I need to do?
- Do I have a checklist that I can use?

3. PLAN

- Plan the steps needed to finish the task.
- Fill out the checklist that I can use.

4. DO

- Sit down and start working!

Cut this out and use it to remind your child of the steps to follow for strong executive functioning skills and to help create the pathway to easier learning.

www.kandmcenter.com

Copyright ©2011 The K&M Center, Inc.

Dear Parent,

The purpose of the K & M Executive Functioning program is to build your child's skills to work independently. Executive Functioning is the CEO in all of us. Some of us are great at organizing, planning and follow through and others need help. This program is the help you have been looking for.

To ensure the success of this program we need your assistance. We will provide the structure and organization that we want your child to learn; however, we depend on you to ensure that your child completes the homework. To improve your child's Executive Functioning, we have designed checklists for your child. We ask you to look over the check list and see if your child did the assigned work.

We have included a contract for you and your child to sign, signifying your willingness to work as a team to help your child reach higher executive functioning skills.

THE CONTRACT

I, _____, agree to complete the Executive Functioning homework assigned to me. I will allow my parent to review my work and sign it each night.

I, _____, agree to check with my child each night and review and sign his/her executive functioning homework.

We, _____

and_____, agree that building executive functioning skills is valuable. We will help each other remember our agreement. We will also have weekly reality checks with the executive functioning trainer to ensure that everyone is aware of all that is going on.

What is the best way to communicate to send homework and get updates?

Email: _____

Phone: _____

Executive Function Workbook Reward Chart

WEEK 1:

(1) (2) (3) (4)

WEEK 2:

(1) (2) (3) (4)

WEEK 3:

(1) (2) (3) (4)

WEEK 4:

(1) (2) (3) (4)

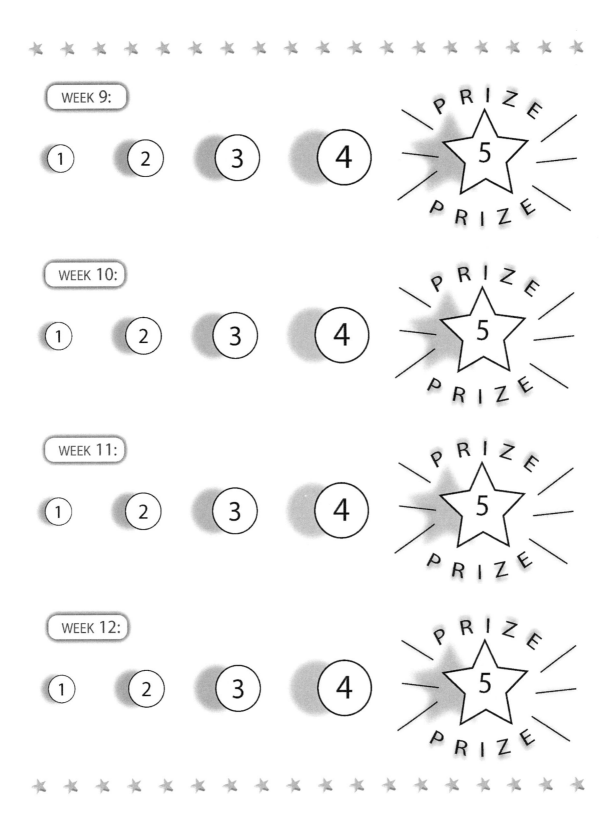

GUIDE TO WORKSHEETS

Use this guide to help you find the pages you find most helpful:

WORKSHEET	PAGE INTRODUCED	WHO DOES WHAT, WHEN	WHY
STUDENT QUESTIONNAIRE	6	Student completes with instructor during 1st session	To determine strengths and weaknesses in executive functioning skills
PARENT EXECUTIVE FUNCTIONING QUESTIONNAIRE	6	Parent completes online by 1st session	Parents takes survey to facilitate conversation with student about executive functioning skills
SETTING YOUR GOALS	10, 32, and throughout workbook	Student completes with instructor during 1st Unit and throughout workbook	Increases student ownership of EF program and schoolwork by setting goals to work toward
STOP THINK PLAN DO	14	Student uses every time they are starting a new task	Encourages metacognition needed to carry out a task
CONTRACT	16	Student and parent sign by 1st session	Both agree to parent's review of Worksheets nightly and check-ins with instructor weekly
PROGRESS CHART	17-19	Student completes with instructor during 1st Unit	Motivates student by tracking progress and adding new goals
STUDENT INTERVIEW	27-31	Student completes with instructor during 2nd Unit	Shows academic strengths and weaknesses; sharpens self-assessment skills
HOW LONG DOES EACH ACTIVITIY TAKE? DAILY CALENDAR SCHEDULING HOMEWORK	37-41	Student completes with instructor during 3rd Unit During 3rd Unit and as needed at home	Student maps available homework/study time each day

WORKSHEET	PAGE INTRODUCED	WHO DOES WHAT, WHEN	WHY
DAILY HOMEWORK PLANNER	43	Student uses daily to plan homework nightly	Documents how well student estimates time needed to do homework
PLANNING TONIGHT'S HOMEWORK	46	Student uses daily to plan homework nightly	Allows student to plan time to complete homework each night
HOMEWORK FLOW CHART	47-48	Student completes with instructor during 4th Unit and daily at home	Breaks down steps to manage multiple assignments every day
BACKPACK CHECKLIST	50-54	Student completes with instructor during 5th Unit and daily at home	Exercises ability to track materials and assignments needed to complete work
STUDY SPACE CHECKLIST	55-57	Student completes with instructor during 5th Unit and at home	Identifies materials needed for schoolwork and arranges purchase and upkeep of these supplies
USING YOUR PLANNER REVIEW PLANNER USE	59-62	Student completes with instructor during 6th Unit and daily at home	Student manages homework/study along with other activities
USING YOUR LONG-TERM PLANNER	67-68	Student completes with instructor during 7th Unit and as needed at home	Breaks down complex assignments into manageable daily tasks
ACTIVE READING QUESTIONS TO ASK ACTIVE READING BOOKMARK	71-72	Student reviews with instructor during 8th Unit and as needed for reading at home	Provides questions to ask yourself when reading at home to help with comprehension

WORKSHEET	PAGE INTRODUCED	WHO DOES WHAT, WHEN	WHY
CHARACTER LIST	73	Student reviews with instructor during 8th Unit and as needed for reading at home	Helps keep track of characters when reading a novel
CHAPTER SUMMARIES	74	Student reviews with instructor during 8th Unit and as needed for reading at home	Summarizes chapters in one sentence to help keep track of the plot of a story
SQ3R READING	75	Student reviews with instructor during 8th Unit and needed for reading at home	Engages student in his/her own learning when reading texts
NOTE-TAKING TIPS	79	Student completes with instructor during 9th Unit and as needed at home	Gives tips for successful note-taking
USE YOUR LONG-TERM PLANNER TO PREPARE FOR TESTS	90-91	Student completes with instructor during 9h Unit and as needed at home	Breaks down review of important material into manageable, ordered tasks

UNIT **2**

CUSTOMIZE THE PROGRAM FOR YOU

YOU WILL BE SEEING THESE SYMBOLS THROUGHOUT THE WORKBOOK:

THEY WILL HELP YOU REMEMBER TO THINK ABOUT YOUR THINKING.

LET'S START NOW!

 STOP: What is this book about? Why are you reading it?

 THINK: It will help you do better in school.

 PLAN: Getting an overview of the book will help you decide which areas will help you most.

DO: Start reading to learn about the program.

OVERVIEW OF THE EXECUTIVE FUNCTIONING BOOK:

THIS BOOK CAN BE COMPLETED IN ANY ORDER YOU WOULD LIKE. WE SUGGEST FLIPPING THROUGH AND FINDING WHICH SECTIONS YOU BELIEVE WILL BE THE MOST HELPFUL AND WORKING THROUGH THOSE FIRST. HERE IS AN OVERVIEW OF EACH OF THE SECTIONS IN THE BOOK:

UNIT 1

WHY LEARN EXECUTIVE FUNCTIONING SKILLS?

This unit will introduce you to the Executive Functioning workbook to explain how it can help you in school. You will take a questionnaire that will help you see some of your strengths as a student as well as some of your challenges.

UNIT 2

CUSTOMIZE THE PROGRAM FOR YOU

In Unit 2, you will see an overview of the program, which can help you decide the best way for you to work through the units.

UNIT 3

HOW MUCH TIME DO I HAVE?

Do you sometimes run out of time when you are doing homework or studying for a test? In this unit, you will be looking at your daily schedule to see how much time you really have each day. It will help you learn to use the time that you do have effectively to get everything finished each day.

UNIT 4

HOMEWORK MADE EASY

Is homework hard for you? In Unit 4, you will learn strategies for planning your daily assignments. It will show you easy ways to make sure you know what you need to complete and how much time it is going to take you.

UNIT 5

HOW TO GET RID OF THE JUNK

When you get home after school are you able to quickly and easily find everything you need in your backpack? Backpack Basics will go over how to free your backpack from all the junk that accumulates and provides checklists to help you keep your backpack in order.

THE POINT OF A PLANNER

Do you ever get home and find that you forgot what pages you had to finish for homework? Unit 6 answers the questions like "Why should I bother using a planner?" and "What do I write in a planner anyway? It also includes checklists that help you monitor your planner to make sure it is doing the best job it can to keep you organized.

STEP BY STEP PLANNING FOR LARGE ASSIGNMENTS

Have you ever found yourself rushing to finish a report the night before it is due? This unit focuses on how to make a plan to complete large, and sometimes overwhelming, assignments. It will give you tools to use that will help you see how many steps you'll need to complete and how you can use your time wisely to finish the project.

WHAT IS ACTIVE READING?

Do you sometime finish reading a passage and realize you don't remember what you just read? Unit 8 will teach you what it means to be an active reader and why that's an important part of being a successful student.

WHY SHOULD I TAKE NOTES?

Have you ever discovered that what was on the test was not in your notes? In this unit, you will learn what it means to be an active listener and why notes are a crucial part of being an involved student. Notes are only useful to you if you know how to do them correctly, and this unit will show you ways to take notes that will really help you.

HOW DO I SHOW WHAT I KNOW ON TESTS?

Don't you hate it when you study for a test only to discover you forgot some important information while taking the test? Once you read a chapter and take good notes, the next step is showing what you know on tests. Unit 10 will give you strategies for being a well-prepared test-taker.

Now THAT YOU'VE SEEN AN OVERVIEW OF ALL THE UNITS, WHICH ONES DO YOU FEEL WILL BE THE MOST HELPFUL FOR YOU?

_____

_____

_____

Start with those three first, then do the rest of the book in any order that you'd like. If you don't have a top 3 list, go ahead and do the book in the order that we have it, starting with Unit 1 and finishing with Unit 10.

NEXT YOU WILL COMPLETE THE INTERVIEW ON THE NEXT PAGE TO HELP YOU DISCOVER SOME OF YOUR STRENGTHS AND WEAKNESSES.

STUDENT INTERVIEW

Have someone ask you these questions and record your answers. Use this as an opportunity to reflect on yourself as a learner to learn more about your strengths and weaknesses. This will help you see which areas would be useful to focus on as you work through the Executive Functioning Workbook.

ENGLISH	
Do you like English?	
Do you consider it a strength or a weakness?	
How is reading? Do you read what is assigned? What are your favorite books? Which books have you disliked?	
Does it take you a long time to get through your reading assignments?	
Do you usually understand the meaning of the literature?	

Do you take notes in your book or mark key passages as you read?	
How is your writing? Do you like to write? Do you type your assignments?	
Does writing take you a long time?	
Do you find it easy or hard to decide what to write about?	
Do you make webs or outlines before writing?	
Do you write a rough draft? Do you make revisions before or after the paper is due?	
What comments do you usually get from your teacher?	

MATH

How's math? Do you consider yourself a good math student?	
What has been your easiest math class? Your hardest?	
Is your homework easy or hard? Do you turn it in on time?	
Do you take notes in class to help you with your homework later?	
How do you prepare for tests? How do you do on tests?	
What kind of errors do you make? Conceptual? Careless?	
What comments do you usually get from your teacher?	

HISTORY	
How about history? Do you consider yourself a good history student?	
Does the reading seem hard?	
How's note-taking in class? On texts?	
How do you do on exams? What comments do you usually get from your teacher? Do you have a preference for short answer, multiple choice or essay tests?	
How do you study for tests? Do you go to review sessions? Study with friends? A tutor?	

SCIENCE	
How's science? Do you consider yourself a good science student?	
What's your favorite part of science? What was your favorite science class? Your least favorite?	
How's your note-taking in class? From texts?	
How do you do on exams? What comments do you usually get from your teacher? Do you have a preference for short answer, multiple choice or essay tests?	
How do you study for tests? Do you go to review sessions? Study with friends? A tutor?	

GOAL SETTING

Now that you have completed the first unit, take some time to think about what you have learned about yourself. Look back to the goals you set for yourself in Unit 1. Did you meet the first goals you set for yourself? If not, should this continue to be a goal for the next week?

Also, take a look at the answers to the interview questions. Do you need to change any of your goals or add new goals? Remember, if you haven't met the goals you set for yourself the first week, these can stay the same. But now is also the time to set any new goals to work through during Unit 2.

MY GOALS:

1. _____

   _____

   _____

2. _____

   _____

   _____

3. _____

   _____

   _____

HOW MUCH TIME DO I HAVE?

LEARNING STRATEGIES FOR BETTER TIME MANAGEMENT

You have probably heard the phrase "time management" over and over in school, but what does it actually mean? Time management means knowing how long something will take and planning the time necessary to complete it.

When planning your time you can use the STOP, THINK, PLAN, DO mantra to help you, along with the checklists in this chapter.

Have you ever had a big project that you thought would take only an hour, so you put it off until the last minute, only to find that it was going to take a lot longer than you thought? Then you probably had to stay up really late finishing it, which ends up being frustrating and tiring.

Underestimating how long activities take can cause lots of frustration, and using the tools in this chapter can help prevent that aggravation.

Sometimes it even feels like there isn't enough time in the day to finish everything we need to finish. The first step is figuring out all of the different activities that make up your day and then deciding how long they each take. That way, you'll be able to map out your schedule to see how much time you REALLY have each day to work on homework, projects, and studying.

WHEN PLANNING MY TIME OR A NEW TASK, I NEED TO:

1. **STOP**

- Stop what I am doing.

2. **THINK**

- What do I need to do?
- Do I have a checklist that I can use?

3. **PLAN**

- Plan the steps needed to finish the task.
- Fill out the checklist that I can use.

4. **DO**

- Start working!

HOW CAN I USE STOP, THINK, PLAN, DO?

These are the steps you will go through each time you start a new task. The more times you walk through these steps, the more automatic the process becomes.

Asking yourself questions as you complete a task will help you take control of your brain – you do this by knowing WHAT questions to ask yourself. This will help you become **metacognitive**, or able to think about your own thinking.

> **METACOGNITIVE:**
> Able to think about your thinking

Here are examples of questions to ask yourself as you move through a project:

1.

QUESTIONS TO ASK MYSELF:

- What should I be doing right now?
- Do I need to stop what I am doing in order to start this new task?

2.

QUESTIONS TO ASK MYSELF:

- What is the teacher asking me to do?
- What do I visualize the final product looking like?
- Do I have a checklist that I can use to help me plan each step?
- What materials will I need?
- Who can I ask for help if I need it?
- Where is the best place to do this project?

3.

PLAN
out the steps
needed to finish

QUESTIONS TO ASK MYSELF:

- What steps do I need to complete in order to finish the project?
- What should I do first?
- What step comes next?
- Did I write all of the steps down in the order I need to complete them?
- How much time will each step take?
- Did I remember to fit in breaks?
- When should I complete each step? (write it down to hold yourself accountable)
- Will I have enough time to finish?

4.

DO
the work I planned
for myself and keep
track of my progress

QUESTIONS TO ASK MYSELF:

- What step am I working on?
- Am I making the progress I should be making?
- Am I staying on task?
- Am I marking off each step as I complete it?
- Is my plan working? If not, how can I improve it?
- Does this look like what I thought it would look like or did I come up with a new idea?

How Accurate is Your Sense of Time?

Estimate how long each of the following activities takes you. Then time yourself doing each one to see how long it *really takes*.

ACTIVITY	HOW LONG DO I THINK IT TAKES?	HOW LONG DID IT *REALLY* TAKE?	WHAT WAS THE DIFFERENCE?
Brushing Your Teeth			
Eating Breakfast			
Getting Dressed and Ready for School			
Eating Dinner			

Now take a look at your estimates. Did you overestimate or underestimate? If you underestimated, that means you are probably not leaving yourself enough time to get things done. Being aware of how long things really take is an important first step in time management, as it allows you to plan the actual amount of time you will need.

Let's move on to another activity that will show you how much of your day is already full with planned activities such as school, sports, and music lessons and how much of your day is left to complete homework, studying, and projects.

WHAT ACTIVITIES FILL UP YOUR DAY?

Use the chart below to fill in how long each activity takes. You will then transfer this information to a weekly chart to keep track of when you will complete each activity. If you are not sure how long an activity takes, use a timer to get a more accurate idea. You might think it only takes you 20 minutes to get ready for school, but once you time it, you may find out it is actually taking closer to an hour.

HOW LONG DOES EACH ACTIVITY TAKE?

DAILY ACTIVITIES	MON	TUE	WED	THU	FRI	SAT	SUN
Getting ready for school							
Getting to school							
Hours in school							
Extracurricular activities (sports, clubs, music, tutoring)							
Getting home from school							
Homework/Studying							
Dinner							
Relaxation-- reading/TV/video games							
Socializing with friends/family							
Last-minute studying							
Getting ready for bed							
Sleeping							
Other							
TOTAL:							

** Remember, there are 24 hours in a day, so each day should equal exactly 24 hours. **

WHAT DOES YOUR SCHEDULE LOOK LIKE?

Now that you have figured out how long each activity takes, you need to determine when you are going to complete each one. Once you make your schedule, you need to stick to it, completing each activity during the time you allot.
1. Mark off on your schedule when you wake up and how much time it takes you to get ready for school.
2. Enter in the time that you are at school each day.
3. Mark off all extracurricular activities – sports, clubs, tutoring, art classes, music, etc. that you do after school. Don't forget to include weekend activities as well.
4. Also mark off the time you eat dinner each night as well as the time you need to be in bed.
5. Now that all of your activities are marked on your schedule, highlight all of your free time in yellow.

	MON	TUE	WED	THU	FRI	SAT	SUN
6:30 a.m.							
7:00							
7:30							
8:00							
1st period							
2nd period							
3rd period							
4th period							
5th period							
6th period							
7th period							
3:00 p.m.							
3:30							
4:00							
4:30							
5:00							
5:30							
6:00							
6:30							
7:00							
7:30							
8:00							
8:30							
9:00							
9:30							
10:00							

Or, if you do not have set class periods each day, you can use this schedule instead to fill in all of your activities.

	MON	TUE	WED	THU	FRI	SAT	SUN
6:30 a.m.							
7:00							
7:30							
8:00							
8:30							
9:00							
9:30							
10:00							
10:30							
11:00							
11:30							
12:00 p.m.							
12:30							
1:00							
1:30							
2:00							
2:30							
3:00							
3:30							
4:00							
4:30							
5:00							
5:30							
6:00							
6:30							
7:00							
7:30							
8:00							
8:30							
9:00							
9:30							
10:00							

QUESTIONS TO ASK MYSELF AFTER FILLING IN MY SCHEDULE

- Is this the amount of free time I thought I had each day?
- How much time do I have each day to complete schoolwork?

MONDAY	
TUESDAY	
WEDNESDAY	
THURSDAY	
FRIDAY	

- Are there any days that I have more time than others? Can I use this day to get ahead on any studying/projects?
- Are there any days that I don't have much time for homework? Are there any assignments that I can do the night before to help make this day more manageable?

UNIT 4

HOMEWORK MADE EASY

Now that you've learned about time management in Unit 3, it's time to apply time management to homework.

- Do you find that you overestimate or underestimate how long homework will take you each night?
- Does it seem that some nights there is just not enough time to get everything done?

By becoming a better estimator of how long assignments will take, you can better plan how long you need to complete homework each night.

Use the Daily Homework Planner on the next page to help see how accurate your estimates are when it comes to homework.

DAILY HOMEWORK PLANNER

You will find directions for using this planner on the next page.

SUBJECT	TASK	ESTIMATED TIME NEEDED	REAL TIME NEEDED	DIFFERENCE

What time will I start my homework tonight?

_____

Make sure to look at your daily schedule and use the time that you have scheduled for homework each day

Based on my time estimates, what time will I be finished?

_____

HOW DO I USE THIS DAILY HOMEWORK PLANNER?——

STOP

- Look at your planner.
- Review your short-term assignments (the ones that are due the next day) and long-term assignments (any projects, tests to study for, etc. that need to be worked on over several days) and write them under tasks.
- If you don't know the homework from one of your classes, call that friend whose number is in your planner.

THINK

- What is due tomorrow? – make sure these come before assignments that are due later in the week
- Which assignments are the hardest? Which are the easiest? – do the harder ones first and save the easier ones for later
- Number the assignments in the order that you plan to do them in.
- Estimate the time it will take for each assignment, asking yourself:
  - How many problems do I have to complete?
  - How long does homework usually take for this class?

PLAN

- Write the amount of time you think each assignment will take under "Estimated time needed."
- Add up the amount of time you estimate your homework will take overall.
- Look at the clock and plan when you are going to start and when you will take breaks. Then estimate when you will be done with your homework. Look at your daily schedule to see how much time you had set aside for homework tonight – do you estimate that you will have enough time to finish it all?

DO

- Set the timer when you start each assignment and stop it when you are finished. Record the actual time for each assignment on your chart. What was the difference?
- Cross off each assignment when it's done!

TIME TO REFLECT

What did you notice about your estimates? Were you accurate, or do you need to start giving yourself more time or less time to complete homework each night? Planning your time to complete both long-term and short-term assignments will make them easier to finish, and you won't find that you are always getting things done at the last minute.

Once you have an accurate idea how long your homework is going to take, you can begin planning other activities without worrying that you aren't leaving enough time for homework.

Once you start becoming a good estimator of how long assignments will take, you can start to use this homework planner to schedule time to complete each assignment. Some students find that it helps to have a schedule right in front of them so they can see if they are on track with their estimates.

PLAN TONIGHT'S HOMEWORK

TIME	TO DO	DONE
3:00 p.m.		
3:30		
4:00		
4:30		
5:00		
5:30		
6:00		
6:30		
7:00		
7:30		
8:00		
8:30		
9:00		
9:30		
10:00		
10:30 p.m.		

Tonight for homework, I have Math, History and Science and I have time on my schedule from 3-5 pm. Math will take 30 minutes, and I'll schedule that first because it's the hardest. Social Studies is only 3 questions and will take about 30 minutes, so I'll do that next. I'll spend the time that's left studying for my Science test because that's not until Friday.

HOMEWORK FLOW CHART

Follow this chart to help you complete each homework assignment. Use the blank one on the next page for your assignments.

STOP what I am doing.

What do I have to do to finish this assignment?
Finish all problems on page 39 correctly.

Break it into steps
Step 1: Read the directions
Step 2: Look at the operation sign
Step 3: Do the problem
Step 4: Check my work

MONITOR YOUR PROGRESS.

How long will it take me to finish?
About 25 minutes
- Reading directions: 5 mins
- Doing the work: 15 mins
- Checking the work: 5 mins

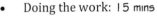 Now DO the work.

EVALUATE.
- How long did it really take? 35 mins
- Did I follow all the directions? yes
- Did I check/ proofread? yes
- Did I check math facts? yes

SUCCEED!
Follow through to the last step.

Put the work in your folder where you put homework, and put the folder in your backpack, and CHECK IT OFF!

HOMEWORK FLOW CHART ————————————

STOP what I am doing.

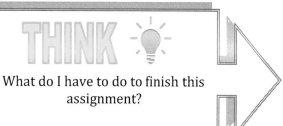

THINK

What do I have to do to finish this assignment?

PLAN

Break it into steps
Step 1:
Step 2:
Step 3:
Step 4:

MONITOR YOUR PROGRESS.

How long will it take me to finish?

- Reading directions:
- Doing the work:
- Checking the work:

Now **DO** the work.

SUCCEED!
Follow through to the last step.

EVALUATE.

- How long did it really take?
- Did I follow all the directions?
- Did I check/ proofread?
- Did I check math facts?

Put the work in your folder where you put homework, and put the folder in your backpack, and CHECK IT OFF!

UNIT 5

BACKPACK BASICS

——————— HOW TO GET RID OF THE JUNK———————

Unit 5 explains why it's important to keep your backpack clean. It may seem like a small thing, but bringing the correct materials to and from school is the only way that you are able to complete homework, have the right materials to study for tests, and bring important things home like binders, books, flash drives, and gym clothes.

There are two times during the day that you should check your backpack:

1. Before you leave home in the morning and
2. Before you leave school in the afternoon.

This way you can check in the morning to make sure you have all the materials you need to bring in to school. Then check in the afternoon as you're leaving to make sure you have everything you need to complete your homework at night.

It may seem silly to stand at your locker and ask yourself "Do I have my planner? Yes. Do I have my binder? Yes." But by using this checklist every day, we start to ask ourselves these questions automatically, which allows us to remember the materials we need to bring back and forth more easily.

You may find it helps to tape the backpack checklist in you locker at school and where you keep your backpack at home to make sure you remember to use it each day.

MORNING CHECKLIST

Before you leave home in the morning, ask yourself:

DO I HAVE...

TO BRING TO SCHOOL	YES, I HAVE IT	NO, I NEED TO GET IT
Planner		
Completed homework -- in my binder for that subject, or in a designated homework folder		
Books, binders, or folders for each subject that I have that day		
Pens and pencils to take notes		
Paper		
Clothing for warmth and after-school activities		
Ask myself: Am I forgetting anything?		
Other materials:		

Do I have my planner? **Yes.**

Do I have my binder? **Yes.**

AFTERNOON CHECKLIST

Before you leave school in the afternoon, ask yourself:

DO I HAVE…

I see I have math homework, so I need to take my math book and spiral notebook.

To Bring Home	Yes, I HAVE IT	No, I NEED TO GET IT
Planner filled out so I know my assignments		
Binders		
ALL books I need to complete homework assignments		
Folders		
Handouts from teachers telling me details about my assignments and upcoming tests		
Slips or notes for parents		
Clothing -- hat, sweater, jacket		
Gym clothes		
Ask myself: Am I forgetting anything?		
Other materials:		

Once you start remembering to bring the correct materials to and from school each day, it's important to keep your backpack clean and organized so you can easily find the materials that you need.

Each day, when you get home from school, you should take everything out of your backpack to GET RID OF THE JUNK. This means taking out old papers and filing them in the correct place, throwing away old lunches, putting gym clothes in the laundry, and putting that extra calculator you've been looking for away where it belongs.

Once you get in the habit of cleaning your backpack every day, it should only take a few minutes. Using this quick checklist will help remind you what to look for:

To Do	Done
Clean out backpack and toss out garbage.	☐
Put pencils and pens in container or zipped compartment.	☐
File all papers in my binders/folders.	☐
Make sure homework is where it belongs.	☐
Put parent handout materials in binder or folder.	☐

If it's easier for you to use a weekly checklist to keep track of your backpack, use the one below. Make sure you are really checking off which things you completed, so you have a way to monitor your progress.

WEEKLY BACKPACK CHECKLIST

Every day, check off each backpack organization task you have completed.

TO BRING TO SCHOOL	M	T	W	TH	F	S/S
Completed homework--in my binder for that subject, or in a designated homework folder						
Books, binders/folders for each subject that I have that day						
Pens and pencils to take notes						
Paper						
Planner						
Clothing for warmth and after-school activities						
Other						
Ask myself: Am I forgetting anything?						

TO BRING HOME	M	T	W	TH	F	S/S
Binders						
Books						
Folders						
Planner filled out so I know my assignments						
Handouts from teachers telling me details about my assignments and upcoming tests						
Slips or notes for parents						
Clothing--hat, sweater, jacket						
Gym clothes						
Other						
Ask myself: Am I forgetting anything?						

BACKPACK ORGANIZATION	M	T	W	TH	F	S/S
Cleaned out backpack and tossed out garbage						
Pencils and pens in container or zipped compartment						
Assignment section or planner						
All papers filed in my binders/folders						
Designated sections for my homework--either a separate folder, or in a binder with dividers						
Parent handout section or folder						

SIGN OFF EACH NIGHT

	M	T	W	TH	F	S/S
STUDENT						
PARENT						

ORGANIZING YOUR STUDY SPACE

Along with an organized backpack, it is also important to keep your study space tidy and stocked with supplies so you can quickly find any materials you need in order to complete your homework each night.

But first, think of the place at home that you use most often to study. If you don't already have a consistent place, now is the time to pick one. Using one study space helps to keep all of your school materials in one place so it's easier to stay organized. Have you thought of the place where you do or will start to do most of your homework and studying?

Go through the checklist below to see if this seems like a good choice.

STUDY SPACE CHECKLIST

MY CHOICE OF A STUDY SPACE: _____

PHYSICAL SPACE	HAVE	NEED
A specific space to study		
A good work surface and chair		
Area to file papers and organize books (cupboard, desk, or file cabinet)		
Good lighting		
Quiet		
Freedom from interruptions		

What did you find? Does this study space have all of the qualities you need in order to get your work done? If not, think of another place that might be better. Use the checklist again to make sure the new place has everything that you'll need.

Now, let's take a look at the materials you may need each night. If you have all of the things you need in one place, you won't need to get up in the middle of doing homework to go find a pencil, calculator, or piece of paper, which will help save you time. There may be some things on this list that you don't need regularly, so don't worry about those materials. Just make sure you have everything that YOU need to complete your homework each night.

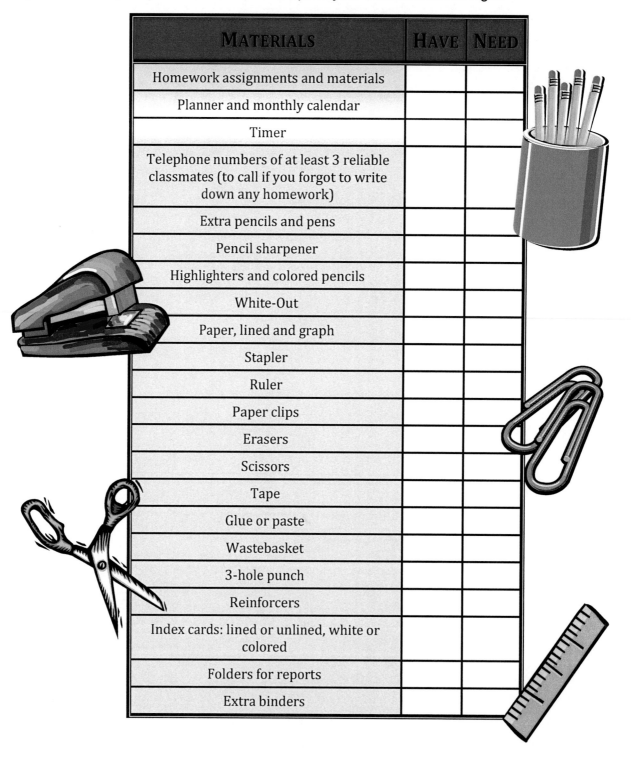

MATERIALS	HAVE	NEED
Homework assignments and materials		
Planner and monthly calendar		
Timer		
Telephone numbers of at least 3 reliable classmates (to call if you forgot to write down any homework)		
Extra pencils and pens		
Pencil sharpener		
Highlighters and colored pencils		
White-Out		
Paper, lined and graph		
Stapler		
Ruler		
Paper clips		
Erasers		
Scissors		
Tape		
Glue or paste		
Wastebasket		
3-hole punch		
Reinforcers		
Index cards: lined or unlined, white or colored		
Folders for reports		
Extra binders		

MATERIALS	HAVE	NEED
Dividers		
Small accordion file		
Dictionary		
Thesaurus		
Calculator		
Computer		
Computer paper		
Is there anything else that you know you will need?		

Use this list as a shopping list and make sure to get these items.
- Who will get what you need?
- When will the items be purchased?

Make sure to keep your study space clean and stocked with materials. After you complete your nightly backpack checklist, quickly check over your study space to make sure everything is put away and ready to go for the next night.

THE POINT OF A PLANNER

Unit 6 discusses why planners are such an important part of being a successful student. You need a planner in order to write down homework so you can remember what to do each night, but there are so many other things that they can help you with.

- Writing down upcoming tests and quizzes helps you know when you need to start studying.
- Writing down a project due date reminds you when it's due.
- You can also use it to keep track of other important dates, such as birthdays, club meetings, and field trips.

It is best to use the planner that your school provides, if that's an option. If your school does not provide a planner, then there are some important points to consider when selecting one.

DOES THE PLANNER HAVE...
☐ ...a daily calendar with enough space to write down all assignments by subjects?
☐ ...enough space to write all assignments neatly?
☐ ...an area for important phone numbers?
☐ ...a full-year calendar?
☐ ...a monthly calendar?

Once you have a planner, you need to know how to use it effectively. A planner can't help you if it travels back and forth to school but has nothing written in it. Remember that your planner is your tool to help you remember everything you need to do. We sometimes think we'll remember everything, such as when our teacher tells us what our math homework is for the night, but by the time we get home, we have forgotten what page we've been assigned. Use this guide to help you decide if you are using your planner correctly, and if not, how you can improve.

HOW TO USE MY PLANNER:
WHAT NEEDS TO GET WRITTEN IN MY PLANNER?

CHECK OFF ANY OF THESE THAT YOU ARE ALREADY WRITING DOWN

☐ ALL homework assignments, including pages and problem numbers

☐ Due dates for projects and papers

☐ Test and quiz dates

☐ Extracurricular activities, such as clubs, sports games, and student council

☐ After school activities, like tutoring, piano, and art classes

☐ Study group and review sessions

☐ Meetings with teachers

Is everything written down that I need to do tonight and this week?

Do I have all of the materials that I need?

Look at any of these that you are not yet writing down. Will it be easier to remember what you have to do once you start recording these in your planner each day?

Now, let's discuss when you need to check your planner during the day. A planner is something that needs to go back and forth from home to school each day as well as to all of your classes.

	CHECK OFF ANY OF THE TIMES THAT YOU ARE ALREADY CHECKING YOUR PLANNER	
☐	BEFORE LEAVING FOR SCHOOL IN THE MORNING...	to make sure you have everything you need for the day
☐	AT THE BEGINNING OF EACH CLASS...	to see if you have anything to turn in
☐	AT THE BEGINNING, MIDDLE, AND END OF CLASS...	to see if there are any new assignments written on the board that you need to write in your planner
☐	BEFORE YOU LEAVE SCHOOL IN THE AFTERNOON...	to make sure you have all of the materials and homework you will need to complete
☐	BEFORE YOU LEAVE SCHOOL IN THE AFTERNOON...	to plan out your homework schedule and fill in your daily homework checklist
☐	BEFORE YOU GO TO BED...	to make sure you did all of your homework and have put all of your materials back in your backpack

That may seem like a lot of times to check your planner each day, but the more you do it, the more of a habit it will become. You'll find that once you start using your planner more effectively, the less often you forget a book in your locker that you need for homework or do the wrong page of math homework because you couldn't remember what your teacher said in class.

11 Tuesday

MATH	pg. 124 #1-19 odds
	Problem of the week due Friday
ENGLISH	Finish comma worksheet
	Read chapter 12 in book
SCIENCE	complete final draft of Lab
HISTORY	test next Thursday
SPANISH	none
OTHER	bring permission slip
	back for field trip

OCTOBER 2011

SUN	MON	TUES	WED	THURS	FRI	SAT
30	31					1
2	3	4	5	6	7	8
9	10	11	12	13	14	15
16	17	18	19	20	21	22
23	24	25	26	27	28	29

Now here's a final checklist to make sure you are using your planner effectively:

CHECK OFF WHICH OF THESE YOU RECORDED IN YOUR PLANNER EACH DAY	M	T	W	TH	F	S/S
ALL homework assignments, including pages and problem numbers						
Due dates for projects and papers						
Test and quiz dates						
Extracurricular activities, such as clubs, sports games, and student council						
After school activities, like tutoring, piano, and art classes						
Study group and review sessions						
Meetings with teachers						

CHECK YOUR PLANNER AT REGULAR TIMES	M	T	W	TH	F	S/S
Before leaving for school in the morning						
At the beginning of each class to see what needs to be turned in						
At the beginning, middle and end of class to write new assignments in my planner						
At the end of the day before you leave school to make sure you know what your assignments are and that you have all the materials that you need						
When you get home, to plan your homework						
When you finish each assignment *(Check it off in your planner.)*						
Before you go to bed *(Check your planner to make sure you did all your homework and have put all your materials back in your backpack.)*						

STEP BY STEP PLANNING FOR LARGE ASSIGNMENTS

When working on long-term assignments such as essays, book reports, or science projects, it can be hard to figure out how much you have to do each night in order to finish on time. The key to this is breaking down a big project into smaller, manageable steps and planning when you'll complete each part.

Before doing this, however, make sure to put the due date on your monthly calendar. Now ask yourself:

- How long do you have to do this project?
- Is it something that you will have to work on during one-week, or will you have the whole month to complete it?

Determine how many days you have, and then start planning when you'll finish each step.

MAY						
M	T	W	T	F	S	S
	1	2	3	4	5	6
7	8	9	10	11	12	13
14	15	16	17	18	19	20
21	22	23	24	25	26	27
28	29	30	31			

STEPS FOR PLANNING OUT ESSAYS, PROJECTS, AND REPORTS

Remember to use your STOP, THINK, PLAN, DO questions from Unit 1 to ask yourself the right questions as you go along.

- Read the directions.
- Make sure you understand the assignment.

- When is it due?
- What steps do you need to complete in order to finish the assignment?
- What do you need to do first?

- Plan the steps needed to finish the task.
- Fill in your checklist.
- Decide when you will complete each step and how long it will take.
- Write in the steps on your monthly calendar

- Start working.
- Follow your schedule.
- Make sure to check off each step as you complete it.

LONG-TERM PLANNER

Assignment/Test: History Research Paper on Civil War

Due date: in 2 ½ weeks (Assigned: Sept. 6th Due: Sept. 22nd)

WHAT DO I NEED TO GET DONE?	HOW LONG WILL IT TAKE?	WHEN WILL I DO IT?	CHECK WHEN DONE!
STEP 1: Read assignment and pick topic	1 hr	Tues. 9/6	☐
STEP 2: Go to library (get books) and search web for information	3 hrs	Sat. 9/10	☐
STEP 3: Read material and take notes	5 hrs	Sun. 9/11 - 2 hrs	☐
		Mon. 9/12 - 1 hr	☐
		Tues. 9/13 - 1 hr	☐
		Wed. 9/14 - 1 hr	☐
STEP 4: Organize material and do outline	3 hrs	Sat. 9/17	☐
STEP 5: Write draft	3 hrs	Sun. 9/18	☐
STEP 6: Edit draft	1 hr	Mon. 9/19	☐
STEP 7: Have parent or teacher review		Tues. 9/20	☐
STEP 8: Make revisions	1 hr	Wed. 9/21	☐
STEP 9: Turn it in!		Thurs. 9/22	☐

What do I have to do first? Pick my topic. Then, I need to get books and research.

MONTHLY CALENDAR

Assignment/Test: History Research Paper on Civil War

Due date: In 2 ½ weeks (Assigned: Sept. 6th Due: Sept. 22nd)

SEPTEMBER 2011

SUNDAY	MONDAY	TUESDAY	WEDNESDAY	THURSDAY	FRIDAY	SATURDAY
				1	2	3
4	5	6 Read assignment and pick topic	7	8	9	10 Go to library to get books and search web for info
11 Read materials and take notes	12 Read materials and take notes	13 Read materials and take notes	14 Read materials and take notes	15	16	17 Organize material and do outline
18 Write draft	19 Edit draft	20 Have parent or teacher review	21 Make revisions	22 Turn it in!	23	24
25	26	27	28	29	30	

Use this blank checklist any time you have a large assignment that you need to break down.

Assignment/Test: _____

Due date: _____

WHAT DO I NEED TO GET DONE?	HOW LONG WILL IT TAKE?	WHEN WILL I DO IT?	CHECK WHEN DONE!
STEP 1:			☐
STEP 2:			☐
STEP 3:			☐
STEP 4:			☐
STEP 5:			☐
STEP 6:			☐
STEP 7:			☐
STEP 8:			☐
STEP 9:			☐

Once you have broken down the project into steps, planned how long each step will take, and planned when you will complete it, transfer each step onto your monthly calendar. Make sure your monthly calendar is hanging somewhere that you check frequently so you can stay on track.

Assignment/Test: _____

Due date: _____

SEPTEMBER 2011

SUNDAY	MONDAY	TUESDAY	WEDNESDAY	THURSDAY	FRIDAY	SATURDAY
				1	2	3
4	5	6	7	8	9	10
11	12	13	14	15	16	17
18	19	20	21	22	23	24
25	26	27	28	29	30	

TIME TO REFLECT ————————

1. How neat is your backpack?

   - Have you been using the backpack checklist each week?
   - What improvements have you seen?
   - Are there any areas you would like to improve on?

BACKPACK ORGANIZATION	M	T	W	TH	F	S/S
Cleaned out backpack and tossed out garbage						
Pencils and pens in container or zipped compartment						
Assignment section or planner						
All papers filed in my binders/folders						
Designated sections for my homework--either a separate folder, or in a binder with dividers						
Parent handout section or folder						

2. How is your planner looking?

   Are you writing everything down?

   - ALL homework assignments, including pages and problem numbers
   - Due dates for projects and papers
   - Test and quiz dates
   - Extracurricular activities, such as clubs, sports games, and student council
   - After school activities, like tutoring, piano, and art classes
   - Study group and review sessions
   - Meetings with teachers

   Are you checking your planner throughout the day?

11   Tuesday

MATH	pg. 124 #1-19 odds
	Problem of the week due Friday
ENGLISH	Finish comma worksheet
	Read chapter 12 in book
SCIENCE	complete final draft of Lab
HISTORY	test next Thursday
SPANISH	none
OTHER	bring permission slip
	back for field trip

OCTOBER 2011

SUN	MON	TUES	WED	THURS	FRI	SAT
30	31					1
2	3	4	5	6	7	8
9	10	11	12	13	14	15
16	17	18	19	20	21	22
23	24	25	26	27	28	29

WHAT IS ACTIVE READING?

Active reading strategies are things can be used while reading textbooks, novels, and handouts that help us get the most from our reading. Educators have found that being actively involved in what you are reading allows you to understand and remember what you have read.

Active reading uses several of the Executive Functioning skills that we have talked about in earlier units, including:

 ## PLANNING

Before reading an assignment, it's important to think about what you want to get out of reading the passage.

- Ask yourself:
  - Why am I reading this passage?
  - What information about the topic do I already know?
  - Can I make any predictions about what I am going to read?

 ## MONITORING

While you are reading, you want to make sure you understand the text. Otherwise, what's the point of reading it?

- Ask yourself:
  - What was the main idea of that section?
  - What are the key vocabulary terms?
  - Can I summarize what I just read?

When reading a book for school, there are things you should do BEFORE, DURING, and AFTER reading to make sure that you understand the material. This is most useful to use when reading books with a plot line, such as novels.

BEFORE

- Ask: "What am I supposed to be getting out of this reading?"
- Preview: skim, look at pictures/captions, timelines
- Look at chapter titles: What do these tell me about the book?
- Predict: "What will the reading will be about?"
- Think: "Have I read anything like this before?"
- Prepare: decide on what note-taking format you will use

DURING

- Take notes in the book or underline/highlight important information.
  - Who are the important characters/people?
  - What are the most important events in each chapter?
- Think, "Can I briefly summarize what I just read?"
- Make a list of characters and describe each.
- Make connections: "Have I ever felt that way before?" or "Have I read/seen something similar to this before?"
- Highlight new vocabulary words
  - Jot them down on a vocabulary list, and make sure to look them up.

AFTER

- Review the vocabulary terms you wrote down. Do you know all of these words now or do you need to review?
- Reread your chapter summary list – can you give a verbal summary of the book?
- What was the conflict, or problem, in the book?
- How did they resolve the conflict?
- Think, "What did I like most about this book? What did I not like about this book?"
- Reflect on how you did with the reading. (see the checklist on the final page of Unit 8)

TOOLS TO USE FOR ACTIVE READING:

Books with a Story Line

The first tool to use is a bookmark to keep your place while you are reading. It has important questions that you should be asking yourself as you read each chapter.

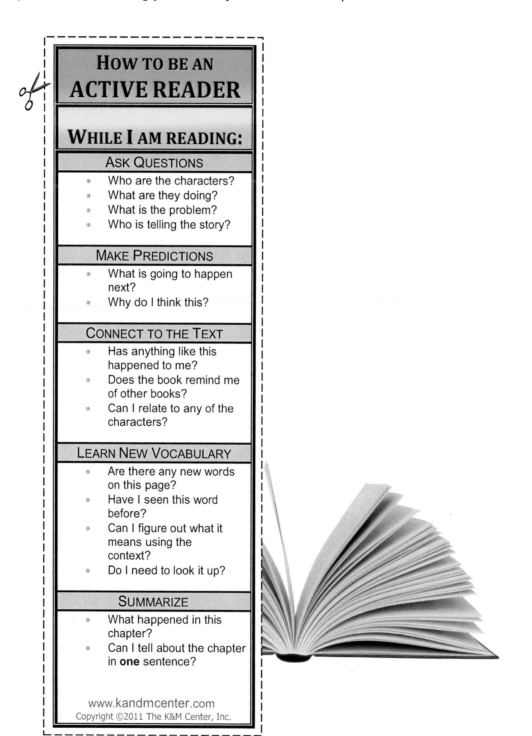

HOW TO BE AN ACTIVE READER

WHILE I AM READING:

ASK QUESTIONS

- Who are the characters?
- What are they doing?
- What is the problem?
- Who is telling the story?

MAKE PREDICTIONS

- What is going to happen next?
- Why do I think this?

CONNECT TO THE TEXT

- Has anything like this happened to me?
- Does the book remind me of other books?
- Can I relate to any of the characters?

LEARN NEW VOCABULARY

- Are there any new words on this page?
- Have I seen this word before?
- Can I figure out what it means using the context?
- Do I need to look it up?

SUMMARIZE

- What happened in this chapter?
- Can I tell about the chapter in **one** sentence?

www.kandmcenter.com
Copyright ©2011 The K&M Center, Inc.

CHARACTER LIST

Use this to help you keep track of characters as you are reading.

CHARACTER'S NAME	DESCRIPTION	WHY ARE THEY IMPORTANT IN THE STORY?

CHAPTER SUMMARIES

Use this to jot down several important events in a chapter.

This way, if you have to write a summary, it is much easier to remember the big events in the book. Use as many copies of this page as you need, until you've completed one for each chapter.

CHAPTER _____:

-
-
-

CHAPTER _____:

-
-
-

CHAPTER _____:

-
-
-

CHAPTER _____:

-
-
-

CHAPTER _____:

-
-
-

CHAPTER _____:

-
-
-

When reading textbooks, like you use in Science and Social Studies, you have to use a different active reading strategy. One proven method to help you understand and remember texts is a strategy called **SQ3R**.

This stands for

SURVEY, QUESTION, READ, RECITE, REVIEW.

S Q 3R

SURVEY:	• The title, headings, and subheadings • Captions under pictures, charts, graphs or maps • Review questions or study guides • Introductory and concluding paragraphs • Summary
QUESTION WHILE YOU ARE SURVEYING:	• Turn the title, headings and/or subheadings into questions to yourself. • Read questions at the end of the chapters or after each subheading. • Ask yourself, "What did my instructor say about this chapter or subject when it was assigned?" • Ask yourself, "What do I already know about this subject?"
READ:	• Look for answers to your questions. • Slow down for hard-to-understand information. • Look for all visual cues in the book: charts, graphs, diagrams, words in bold.
RECITE:	• When you find the answers to your questions, tell yourself or someone the answers. • Restate the question, then give your answer. • Underline or highlight the answers to your questions.
REVIEW:	• Write key words from your questions next to your highlighted information.
REVIEW FOR THE TEST:	• Go back and reread only the highlighted sections. • Use the key words in the margin to check your memory for the main ideas. • Make flashcards for any information you have trouble remembering. • Test and retest yourself on this information using your notes and flashcards.

TIME TO REFLECT

After you read, it's important to reflect on your process to see what worked well and what changes you want to make for next time.

You can use this checklist to help you reflect on your reading:

DID I...	
READ AS MANY PAGES AS I WAS SUPPOSED TO READ?	☐
USE ACTIVE READING STRATEGIES TO HELP ME UNDERSTAND?	☐
• Preview the text	☐
• Take notes/use the active reading tools	☐
• Use the active reading bookmark	☐
STAY FOCUSED ON MY READING WITHOUT GETTING DISTRACTED?	☐
UNDERSTAND WHAT I READ?	☐

OTHER QUESTIONS TO ASK MYSELF:

• What active reading strategies did I use today?

• Is there anything that I can do better next time?

WHY SHOULD I TAKE NOTES?

Active reading, as you learned about in the last unit, is one part of being an involved student. Taking notes is another important part of being a good student. Using active reading and learning note-taking strategies will help you to remember the information that you are reading or listening to and is a great way to prepare for tests.

Have you ever gone to study for a test and realized that you hadn't taken any notes to help you? Then you are stuck going back to reread large sections of your textbook, which can take more time than you have.

By learning good note-taking strategies and using them both in class when your teacher is lecturing and at home when you are reading on your own will help you to better learn and remember the information you are learning.

Remember to use your STOP, THINK, PLAN, DO questions from Unit 1 to ask yourself the right questions as you go along.

- Are you going to be taking notes on a lecture or on a reading assignment?

- What unit are we studying now?
- What topic is the reading or lecture going to cover?
- What do I already know about this topic?

- What is going to be the best note-taking format to use?
- What materials do I need? (book, highlighter, etc.)

- Take notes.
- Think, is this the best note-taking technique to use or do I need to try another way?

NOTE-TAKING TIPS

- **U**se a loose-leaf notebook, or binder, so you can add in pages.

- **W**rite the subject, date, and topic on the top of the page.

- **S**eparate the main idea from the details.

- **U**se as few words as possible. Try to use bullet points and abbreviations to keep things short.

- **U**se your own words. If taking notes on a book, don't copy anything directly from the book.

- **U**nderline or highlight important information.

- **G**o over your notes after you take them – make sure you understand what you've written.

- **W**rite any questions you have, and edit your notes to be clear.

- **S**ummarize the most important information.

- **W**rite down key words or phrases to remember.

HOW DO I FORMAT MY NOTES?

DIVIDE YOUR PAGE

One format is to divide your page into main ideas and supporting details.

1. First, fold your paper into a 1/3 section on the left and a 2/3 section on the right.

2. Then, write the main ideas from the lecture on the left side of the page and the supporting details on the right.

Main Idea	Supporting Details
	•
	•
	•
Main Idea	Supporting Details
	•
	•
	•
Main Idea	Supporting Details
	•
	•
	•

Summary of what is covered on this page of notes

MAKE AN OUTLINE

Another format is to make an outline. An outline also separates the main idea from the supporting details.

EXAMPLE:

Richard Meier

Richard Meier is a world renowned American architect who completed a majority of his most famous work in the 1970s and 1980s. He was born in Newark, New Jersey on October 12, 1934. Meier received his degree in architecture from Cornell University in 1957, at which point he travelled to Europe in hopes of learning from the then-prominent Mid-Century Modern designers. After two years, Meier returned to New York where he worked for several architecture firms until 1963 when he began working with four other prominent American architects- Peter Eisenman, Charles Gwathmey, Michael Graves, and John Hejduk. The five men became known as the "New York Five" and were celebrated for their innovative, playful and unique designs.

Although Meier's work is considered to be in the Post Modern style, his largest architectural influences were Mid-Century Modern designers such as LeCorbusier and Mies Van Der Rohe. When designing his homes and buildings, Meier focuses largely on space, form and light, and the manipulation of each to emphasize a structure's surroundings. In fact, Meier's methods and philosophy regarding the use of form to create light and shadow to define space continues to inspire and influence architects today.

Upon seeing Richard Meier's work, it is easy to see the basic themes of space, form and light play out. It is also apparent as you view his work chronologically that, while his earlier work seemed to have some of the more boxy, purist influence typical of the Mid-Century Modern style, Meier eventually seems to become a bit more playful in his designs. While Meier has a bountiful portfolio of exceptional work, perhaps his three most famous buildings include The Getty Center in Los Angeles, The Barcelona Museum of Contemporary Art, and The Atheneum in New Harmony, Indiana.

1) **M**ain idea
   a) Supporting detail
   b) Supporting detail
   c) Supporting detail

2) **M**ain idea
   a) Supporting detail
   b) Supporting detail
   c) Supporting detail

3) **M**ain idea
   a) Supporting detail
   b) Supporting detail
   c) Supporting detail

1) Richard Meier- world famous American Architect
   a) 1957- graduated Cornell University
   b) 1963- began work with the "New York Five"
   c) Most famous work done in the 1970s-1980s

2) The focus of Meier's building and home design:
   a) Space
   b) Form
   c) Light

3) 3 most famous works:
   a) The Getty Center in Los Angeles
   b) The Barcelona Museum of Contemporary Art
   c) The Atheneum in New Harmony, Indiana

In classes where you are learning about events in chronological order, a timeline would be a helpful note-taking strategy to use. This can be used when reading a history textbook, a science textbook, or even a novel.

1. Write the starting date on the left side.

2. Write specific facts to the right, and continue listing dates and facts until the time sequence is complete.

1776	1812	1861-1865
Declaration of Independence	War with Great Britain	American Civil War

While you can easily make a timeline while reading a textbook, it is a little more difficult to make a timeline while your teacher is lecturing. If he or she begins talking about a lot of dates and facts, you might want to take out a blank sheet of paper to begin making a timeline. Another idea would be to have a copy of a blank timeline and take it out when you need it.

DRAW A GRAPHIC ORGANIZER OR CONCEPT MAP ————————————

Sometimes, using a concept map is helpful in organizing the information we are taking notes on.

When drawing a concept map:

- Make sure to work in pencil so you can add or delete information.
- Think about the information you want to cover in your notes.
- Write the main idea in the center of the page and circle or box it.
- As you read or listen, add the next concept given.
- Connect details to the main idea with lines, and draw a circle around each connected idea.

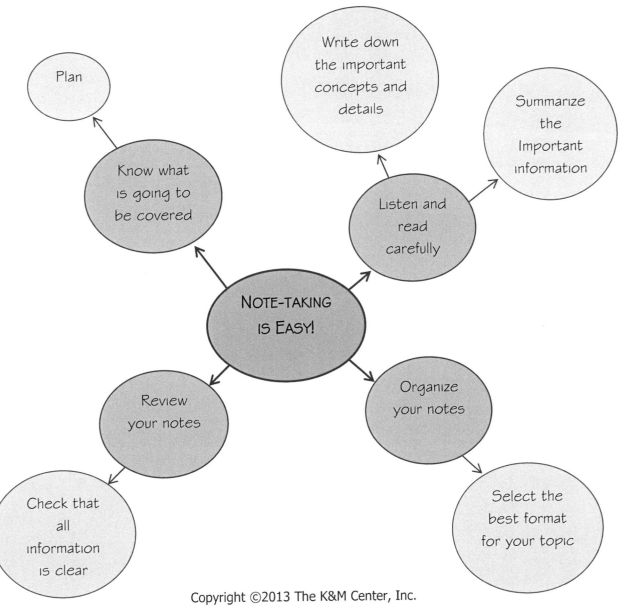

STUDYING FOR TESTS

It is time to start applying everything you have learned about executive functioning to taking tests. Many students feel anxious about taking tests. It can be nerve-wracking to take a test surrounded by other students, feeling pressured to finish in a set amount of time, and knowing that you will be graded on your performance. The good news is that the best remedy for test anxiety is PREPARATION.

What's the best way to prepare for a test? Consider that most topics presented in class will be covered on a future test. Therefore, students who listen actively in class, take good notes, and complete homework are **already preparing** for tests. Your studying starts as soon as class begins.

Let's reflect back on the last week:
- What tests did you have this week?
- How did you do on them?
- What study techniques worked the best for you? Why?
- Did you feel prepared for your tests?
- Were you calm?

Sometimes, students think they have prepared for a test if they just reread their notes 10 minutes before the test. But remember, studying for tests is a process that starts in class.

> ## GOOD STUDYING
> ## means that you have been:
>
> - Attending classes
> - Actively listening and taking notes
> - Reviewing your notes regularly
> - Keeping up with assigned reading and taking notes on it
> - And, most important, **reviewing your notes from lectures and texts before each class**

STEPS TO PREPARE FOR A TEST

Now, you might be asking yourself, "How do I actually study for a test?" The tips below are things to keep in mind when preparing to take a test:

- LISTEN TO THE TEACHER AND TAKE GOOD NOTES.

- ORGANIZE THE MATERIALS THAT WILL BE ON THE TEST.
  - THIS MEANS PUTTING YOUR NOTES IN ORDER BY DATE, KEEPING CLASS HANDOUTS TOGETHER, AND KNOWING WHAT MATERIAL WILL BE COVERED ON THE TEST.

- REVIEW PAST TESTS AND QUIZZES TO SEE THE TYPES OF QUESTIONS THE TEACHER ASKS AND THE TYPES OF ERRORS YOU MAKE.

- NOTE WHAT KIND OF TEST IT WILL BE: OPEN-NOTE, MULTIPLE CHOICE, OR ESSAY.
  - REMEMBER THERE ARE DIFFERENT STRATEGIES TO USE FOR EACH TYPE OF TEST, SO KNOWING IN ADVANCE WHAT KIND OF TEST IT WILL BE CAN HELP GUIDE YOUR STUDYING.

- REVIEW WHAT STUDY STRATEGIES HAVE WORKED BEST FOR YOU IN THIS CLASS.

- TO PLAN YOUR STUDY TIME, FILL OUT YOUR PLANNER, STARTING WITH THE DATE OF THE TEST AND WORK BACKWARDS. SCHEDULE WHAT TOPICS YOU WILL REVIEW, HOW LONG EACH WILL TAKE, AND THE DATES AND TIMES YOU WILL REVIEW EACH.

- WRITE DOWN AND SCHEDULE THE TASKS FOR EACH STEP OF YOUR REVIEW.
  - FOR EXAMPLE, WILL YOU BE READING OVER YOUR NOTES, CREATING A TIMELINE, MAKING FLASHCARDS WITH KEY VOCABULARY TERMS, ETC.

- SAVE THE NIGHT BEFORE THE TEST FOR REVIEWING, NOT LEARNING NEW MATERIAL.
  - YOU SHOULD NEVER TRY TO LEARN ALL OF THE MATERIAL THE NIGHT BEFORE. THIS NIGHT SHOULD BE SAVED FOR A FINAL REVIEW SO YOU GO INTO THE TEST FEELING CONFIDENT.

QUESTIONS TO ASK YOURSELF
BEFORE TAKING A TEST

- Do I understand the directions?
- Will I lose points for mistakes?
- How much time do I have for each section?

STEPS TO FOLLOW
DURING A TEST

- Before you write anything, read the directions carefully.

- Survey the entire test to get the big picture before you begin.

- Determine what kind/kinds of questions you are being asked:
  - *Multiple Choice*
  - *True/False*
  - *Short Answer*
  - *Essay*
  - *Math*

- Budget your time for each section of the test.

- Slow down and calm yourself throughout the test.

- Review the test thoroughly before you turn it in.

QUESTIONS TO ASK YOURSELF
AFTER TAKING A TEST

- Did I do as well on the test as I thought I did?
- What mistakes did I make?
- Did I study the right material and use my study time effectively?
- Is there anything I can improve on next time?

TIPS FOR STUDYING FOR SPECIFIC TYPES OF TESTS

There are certain strategies to follow when taking different types of tests. See the hints below to help you succeed with each kind of assessment.

STEPS TO FOLLOW FOR MULTIPLE CHOICE TESTS

1. Read the directions carefully.

2. Read the questions first while covering the answers. Try to answer the question and then look at the choices to see if your answer is there.

3. If your answer is not there, eliminate the ones you know are wrong.

4. Eliminate the answers that don't fit the question grammatically.

5. If two or three options seem equally correct, all of the above may be the right answer.

6. If two options seem to be direct opposites, chances are that one of those is correct.

7. If two options seem correct, compare them for differences. Then go back to the question and find the best answer.

8. Take a guess, unless there is a penalty.

9. Remember to look for the best answer, not just a correct one.

STEPS TO FOLLOW FOR TRUE/FALSE TESTS

1. Look for negatives such as **no**, **not**, or **cannot**, and look for **double negatives**.

   - Reread the question, dropping the negative/s, and see if what remains is true. Then, reinsert the negatives to answer.

   - For example, if a question reads, **It is not sunny today,** drop the **not** to see if the sentence is true, and then reinsert **not** to answer the question.

2. Watch out for absolute words. Most things do not occur in absolutes. When the question contains **no**, **never**, **none**, **always**, **every**, **entirely**, or **only** it increases the chances it will be incorrect, because it has to be 100% true to be correct.

STEPS TO FOLLOW FOR SHORT-ANSWER TESTS

1. While preparing for a short-answer test, focus on the main points rather than on details, so your answers will include the most important points.

2. Highlight your notes to make sure you understand the main idea of the topics you are studying.

3. Be able to express the main idea concisely with one or two supporting details. You may want to use a web to categorize each topic and add the supporting details.

4. While taking a short-answer test, write your answers in concise, meaningful sentences. Pack in as much information as you can.

5. Remember, a good or "educated" guess is better than leaving the item blank.

STEPS TO FOLLOW FOR ESSAY TESTS

1. Manage the time you have to complete the essays. Often essays come at the end of exams, but are worth a lot of points. Leave enough time to plan and complete the essay.

2. Read through the questions first and decide the order in which you will answer them.

3. Pay attention to key words in the question, such as **compare**, **contrast**, and **criticize**.

4. Plan before you write! Do a web or outline, making sure you have evidence for each of your points. Then, decide the order in which you will present your points (for example, most important to least important).

5. Follow good essay-writing rules:

   • Begin with a clear thesis statement.

   • Support your thesis with good evidence.

   • Summarize your points in the conclusion.

   • Reread and edit your work.

STEPS TO FOLLOW FOR MATH TESTS

PREPARING FOR MATH TESTS:

1. Take good notes in class.

2. Do all your homework and make sure you understand the problems. If you do not understand the problems, write down a question to ask your teacher.

3. Meet with your teacher to clarify the concepts.

4. Take practice tests and do chapter review problems to get used to doing problems in different formats and in the amount of time you will have for the test.

DURING MATH TESTS:

1. Read the directions.

2. Talk yourself through each problem.

3. Show every step of your work clearly.

4. Double-check your work along the way.

5. Make sure you are following the correct sign.

6. If you get stuck, go to another problem and return to the hard problem later.

LONG-TERM PLANNER

Use this planner to determine what material you need to study and when you will complete each part. Then, once you've made a plan, make sure to write what you need to do each night on your master calendar.

Subject: Math

Test date: Tuesday 9/20   Assigned: Monday 9/12

What needs to be covered: Adding/subtracting fractions, turning fractions into decimals, percentages

How long do I have to study?: 9 days

WHAT DO I NEED TO GET DONE?	HOW LONG WILL IT TAKE?	WHEN WILL I DO IT?	CHECK WHEN DONE!
STEP 1: Organize Materials	10 min	Mon. 9/12	☐
STEP 2: Make Study Plan	25 min	Mon. 9/12	☐
STEP 3: Review adding fractions – same and different denominators	20-30 min	Tues. 9/13	☐
STEP 4: Review subtracting fractions – same and different denominators	20-30 min	Wed. 9/14	☐
STEP 5: Review turning fractions into decimals	20-30 min	Thurs. 9/15	☐
STEP 6: Review percentages	45 min	Fri. 9/16	☐
STEP 7: Do problems from chapter test/chapter review	1 hour	Sun. 9/18	☐
STEP 8: Review material the night before the test	45 min – 1 hour	Mon. 9/19	☐
STEP 9: Relax and do well on the test		Tues. 9/20	☐

MONTHLY CALENDAR

SEPTEMBER

SUNDAY	MONDAY	TUESDAY	WEDNESDAY	THURSDAY	FRIDAY	SATURDAY
				1	2	3
4	5	6	7	8	9	10
11	12 Organize Materials & Make Study Plan	13 Review adding fractions – same and different denominators	14 Review subtracting fractions – same and different denominators	15 Review turning fractions into decimals	16 Review percentages	17
18 Do problems from chapter test/ chapter review	19 Review material	20 Relax and do well on the test!	21	22	23	24
25	26	27	28	29	30	

EXECUTIVE FUNCTION WORKBOOK CONCLUSION

Now that you've completed all 10 units, take the chance to reflect on your progress through the program and set up some ongoing goals for the future.

Take a minute and rate yourself on a few of the main areas that you have covered:

Rate yourself
a **5** if you are CONSISTENTLY FOLLOWING YOUR PLAN,
a **1** would mean YOU HAVE FORGOTTEN TO FOLLOW THE PLAN

 1. HOW IS YOUR DAILY SCHEDULE GOING?

5 (always) - 1 (never)	DAILY SCHEDULE
	I am sticking with the weekly schedule I created.
	I have enough time each night to complete my homework.
	I am making a To-Do list each night and prioritizing my assignments.
	I am able to break down a long term assignment into smaller steps and follow them.

2. HOW DOES YOUR BACKPACK LOOK?

5 (always) - 1 (never)	BACKPACK
	I am keeping my backpack clean and organized.
	I am bringing the correct materials to and from school each day.
	My materials are staying organized.

3. ARE YOU USING YOUR PLANNER EFFECTIVELY?

5 (always) - 1 (never)	PLANNER
	I am recording my homework each night.
	I am remembering to write down test dates, extracurricular activities, and long-term project due date.

4. ARE YOU APPLYING EXECUTIVE FUNCTIONING SKILLS TO YOUR SCHOOLWORK?

5 (always) - 1 (never)	EXECUTIVE FUNCTIONING SKILLS
	I am using active reading strategies.
	I am taking notes in my classes.
	I am using good study strategies to prepare for tests.

Think of some positive changes you've seen in your work habits and organization. RECORD THEM BELOW:

Now, think about anything that is still challenging.
SET THREE ONGOING GOALS YOU HAVE FOR YOURSELF AND RECORD THEM BELOW:

MY GOALS:

1. _____
_____
_____

2. _____
_____
_____

3. _____
_____
_____

CONGRATULATIONS ON COMPLETING THE EXECUTIVE FUNCTIONING HANDBOOK!

YOU SHOULD BE VERY PROUD OF YOURSELF FOR TAKING THE NECESSARY STEPS TO BECOME A BETTER STUDENT. REMEMBER TO KEEP WORKING HARD AT THESE SKILLS YOU'VE DEVELOPED IN ORDER TO BECOME THE MOST EFFECTIVE AND EFFICIENT LEARNER YOU CAN BE.

APPENDIX

Worksheets to Copy & Use!

GOAL SETTING

Now that you've taken the questionnaire and done some self-reflection, it's time to set some goals for yourself. Keeping in mind your strengths and weaknesses and your answers to the questions above, what do you think are the top three things you'd like to improve in? Remember to make them reasonable – you don't want to set a goal that is impossible to reach.

For example, if you have trouble keeping your binder organized, a goal might be:

> "I will plan 10 minutes every night to clean out loose papers in my binder and file papers that I put in the front pocket."

MY GOALS:

1. _____
   _____
   _____

2. _____
   _____
   _____

3. _____
   _____
   _____

HERE IS WHAT TO THINK ABOUT BEFORE STARTING A NEW TASK:

1. STOP

- Stop what I am doing.

2. THINK

- What do I need to do?
- Do I have a checklist that I can use?

3. PLAN

- Plan the steps needed to finish the task.
- Fill out the checklist that I can use.

4. DO

- Sit down and start working!

Cut this out and use it to remind your child of the steps to follow for strong executive functioning skills and to help create the pathway to easier learning.

www.kandmcenter.com
Copyright ©2011 The K&M Center, Inc.

HOW CAN I USE STOP, THINK, PLAN, DO?

These are the steps you will go through each time you start a new task. The more times you walk through these steps, the more automatic the process becomes.

Asking yourself questions as you complete a task will help you take control of your brain – you do this by knowing WHAT questions to ask yourself. This will help you become **metacognitive**, or able to think about your own thinking.

> **METACOGNITIVE:**
> Able to think about your thinking

Here are examples of questions to ask yourself as you move through a project:

1.
STOP
what I am doing

QUESTIONS TO ASK MYSELF:

- What should I be doing right now?
- Do I need to stop what I am doing in order to start this new task?

2.
THINK
through the project

QUESTIONS TO ASK MYSELF:

- What is the teacher asking me to do?
- What do I visualize the final product looking like?
- Do I have a checklist that I can use to help me plan each step?
- What materials will I need?
- Who can I ask for help if I need it?
- Where is the best place to do this project?

3. **PLAN** out the steps needed to finish

QUESTIONS TO ASK MYSELF:

- What steps do I need to complete in order to finish the project?
- What should I do first?
- What step comes next?
- Did I write all of the steps down in the order I need to complete them?
- How much time will each step take?
- Did I remember to fit in breaks?
- When should I complete each step? (write it down to hold yourself accountable)
- Will I have enough time to finish?

4. **DO** the work I planned for myself and keep track of my progress

QUESTIONS TO ASK MYSELF:

- What step am I working on?
- Am I making the progress I should be making?
- Am I staying on task?
- Am I marking off each step as I complete it?
- Is my plan working? If not, how can I improve it?
- Does this look like what I thought it would look like or did I come up with a new idea?

WHAT DOES YOUR SCHEDULE LOOK LIKE?

Now that you have figured out how long each activity takes, you need to determine when you are going to complete each one. Once you make your schedule, you need to stick to it, completing each activity during the time you allot.

1. Mark off on your schedule when you wake up and how much time it takes you to get ready for school.
2. Enter in the time that you are at school each day.
3. Mark off all extracurricular activities – sports, clubs, tutoring, art classes, music, etc. that you do after school. Don't forget to include weekend activities as well.
4. Also mark off the time you eat dinner each night as well as the time you need to be in bed.
5. Now that all of your activities are marked on your schedule, highlight all of your free time in yellow.

	MON	TUE	WED	THU	FRI	SAT	SUN
6:30 a.m.							
7:00							
7:30							
8:00							
1st period							
2nd period							
3rd period							
4th period							
5th period							
6th period							
7th period							
3:00 p.m.							
3:30							
4:00							
4:30							
5:00							
5:30							
6:00							
6:30							
7:00							
7:30							
8:00							
8:30							
9:00							
9:30							
10:00							

Or, if you do not have set class periods each day, you can use this schedule instead to fill in all of your activities.

	MON	TUE	WED	THU	FRI	SAT	SUN
6:30 a.m.							
7:00							
7:30							
8:00							
8:30							
9:00							
9:30							
10:00							
10:30							
11:00							
11:30							
12:00 p.m.							
12:30							
1:00							
1:30							
2:00							
2:30							
3:00							
3:30							
4:00							
4:30							
5:00							
5:30							
6:00							
6:30							
7:00							
7:30							
8:00							
8:30							
9:00							
9:30							
10:00							

DAILY HOMEWORK PLANNER

You will find directions for using this planner on the next page.

SUBJECT	TASK	ESTIMATED TIME NEEDED	REAL TIME NEEDED	DIFFERENCE

What time will I start my homework tonight?

_____

Make sure to look at your daily schedule and use the time that you have scheduled for homework each day

Based on my time estimates, what time will I be finished?

_____

Once you start becoming a good estimator of how long assignments will take, you can start to use this homework planner to schedule time to complete each assignment. Some students find that it helps to have a schedule right in front of them so they can see if they are on track with their estimates.

PLAN TONIGHT'S HOMEWORK

TIME	TO DO	DONE
3:00 p.m.		
3:30		
4:00		
4:30		
5:00		
5:30		
6:00		
6:30		
7:00		
7:30		
8:00		
8:30		
9:00		
9:30		
10:00		
10:30 p.m.		

Tonight for homework, I have Math, History and Science and I have time on my schedule from 3-5 pm. Math will take 30 minutes, and I'll schedule that first because it's the hardest. Social Studies is only 3 questions and will take about 30 minutes, so I'll do that next. I'll spend the time that's left studying for my Science test because that's not until Friday.

HOMEWORK FLOW CHART ─────

STOP what I am doing.

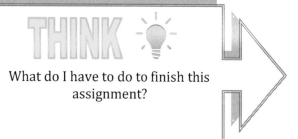
THINK 💡

What do I have to do to finish this assignment?

PLAN

Break it into steps
Step 1:
Step 2:
Step 3:
Step 4:

MONITOR YOUR PROGRESS.

How long will it take me to finish?

- Reading directions:
- Doing the work:
- Checking the work:

Now DO the work.

EVALUATE.

- How long did it really take?
- Did I follow all the directions?
- Did I check/ proofread?
- Did I check math facts?

SUCCEED!
Follow through to the last step.

Put the work in your folder where you put homework, and put the folder in your backpack, and CHECK IT OFF!

MORNING CHECKLIST

Before you leave home in the morning, ask yourself:

DO I HAVE…

TO BRING TO SCHOOL	YES, I HAVE IT	NO, I NEED TO GET IT
Planner		
Completed homework -- in my binder for that subject, or in a designated homework folder		
Books, binders, or folders for each subject that I have that day		
Pens and pencils to take notes		
Paper		
Clothing for warmth and after-school activities		
Ask myself: Am I forgetting anything?		
Other materials:		

Do I have my planner? **Yes.**

Do I have my binder? **Yes.**

A̲FTERNOON̲ C̲HECKLIST

Before you leave school in the afternoon, ask yourself:

D̲O̲ I H̲AVE̲...

> I see I have math homework, so I need to take my math book and spiral notebook.

TO BRING HOME	YES, I HAVE IT	NO, I NEED TO GET IT
Planner filled out so I know my assignments		
Binders		
ALL books I need to complete homework assignments		
Folders		
Handouts from teachers telling me details about my assignments and upcoming tests		
Slips or notes for parents		
Clothing -- hat, sweater, jacket		
Gym clothes		
Ask myself: Am I forgetting anything?		
Other materials:		

Once you start remembering to bring the correct materials to and from school each day, it's important to keep your backpack clean and organized so you can easily find the materials that you need.

Each day, when you get home from school, you should take everything out of your backpack to GET RID OF THE JUNK. This means taking out old papers and filing them in the correct place, throwing away old lunches, putting gym clothes in the laundry, and putting that extra calculator you've been looking for away where it belongs.

Once you get in the habit of cleaning your backpack every day, it should only take a few minutes. Using this quick checklist will help remind you what to look for:

To Do	Done
Clean out backpack and toss out garbage.	☐
Put pencils and pens in container or zipped compartment.	☐
File all papers in my binders/folders.	☐
Make sure homework is where it belongs.	☐
Put parent handout materials in binder or folder.	☐

If it's easier for you to use a weekly checklist to keep track of your backpack, use the one below. Make sure you are really checking off which things you completed, so you have a way to monitor your progress.

WEEKLY BACKPACK CHECKLIST

Every day, check off each backpack organization task you have completed.

TO BRING TO SCHOOL	M	T	W	TH	F	S/S
Completed homework--in my binder for that subject, or in a designated homework folder						
Books, binders/folders for each subject that I have that day						
Pens and pencils to take notes						
Paper						
Planner						
Clothing for warmth and after-school activities						
Other						
Ask myself: Am I forgetting anything?						

TO BRING HOME	M	T	W	TH	F	S/S
Binders						
Books						
Folders						
Planner filled out so I know my assignments						
Handouts from teachers telling me details about my assignments and upcoming tests						
Slips or notes for parents						
Clothing--hat, sweater, jacket						
Gym clothes						
Other						
Ask myself: Am I forgetting anything?						

BACKPACK ORGANIZATION	M	T	W	TH	F	S/S
Cleaned out backpack and tossed out garbage						
Pencils and pens in container or zipped compartment						
Assignment section or planner						
All papers filed in my binders/folders						
Designated sections for my homework--either a separate folder, or in a binder with dividers						
Parent handout section or folder						

SIGN OFF EACH NIGHT

	M	T	W	TH	F	S/S
STUDENT						
PARENT						

Now, let's take a look at the materials you may need each night. If you have all of the things you need in one place, you won't need to get up in the middle of doing homework to go find a pencil, calculator, or piece of paper, which will help save you time. There may be some things on this list that you don't need regularly, so don't worry about those materials. Just make sure you have everything that YOU need to complete your homework each night.

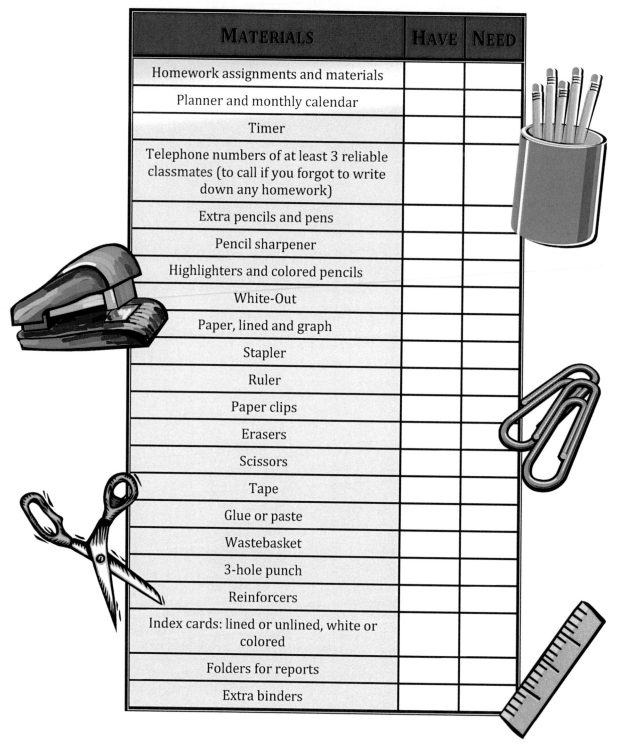

MATERIALS	HAVE	NEED
Homework assignments and materials		
Planner and monthly calendar		
Timer		
Telephone numbers of at least 3 reliable classmates (to call if you forgot to write down any homework)		
Extra pencils and pens		
Pencil sharpener		
Highlighters and colored pencils		
White-Out		
Paper, lined and graph		
Stapler		
Ruler		
Paper clips		
Erasers		
Scissors		
Tape		
Glue or paste		
Wastebasket		
3-hole punch		
Reinforcers		
Index cards: lined or unlined, white or colored		
Folders for reports		
Extra binders		

MATERIALS	HAVE	NEED
Dividers		
Small accordion file		
Dictionary		
Thesaurus		
Calculator		
Computer		
Computer paper		
Is there anything else that you know you will need?		

Use this list as a shopping list and make sure to get these items.
- Who will get what you need?
- When will the items be purchased?

Make sure to keep your study space clean and stocked with materials. After you complete your nightly backpack checklist, quickly check over your study space to make sure everything is put away and ready to go for the next night.

Now here's a final checklist to make sure you are using your planner effectively:

CHECK OFF WHICH OF THESE YOU RECORDED IN YOUR PLANNER EACH DAY	M	T	W	TH	F	S/S
ALL homework assignments, including pages and problem numbers						
Due dates for projects and papers						
Test and quiz dates						
Extracurricular activities, such as clubs, sports games, and student council						
After school activities, like tutoring, piano, and art classes						
Study group and review sessions						
Meetings with teachers						

CHECK YOUR PLANNER AT REGULAR TIMES	M	T	W	TH	F	S/S
Before leaving for school in the morning						
At the beginning of each class to see what needs to be turned in						
At the beginning, middle and end of class to write new assignments in my planner						
At the end of the day before you leave school to make sure you know what your assignments are and that you have all the materials that you need						
When you get home, to plan your homework						
When you finish each assignment (Check it off in your planner.)						
Before you go to bed (Check your planner to make sure you did all your homework and have put all your materials back in your backpack.)						

Use this blank checklist any time you have a large assignment that you need to break down.

Assignment/Test: _____

Due date: _____

WHAT DO I NEED TO GET DONE?	HOW LONG WILL IT TAKE?	WHEN WILL I DO IT?	CHECK WHEN DONE!
STEP 1:			☐
STEP 2:			☐
STEP 3:			☐
STEP 4:			☐
STEP 5:			☐
STEP 6:			☐
STEP 7:			☐
STEP 8:			☐
STEP 9:			☐

TOOLS TO USE FOR ACTIVE READING:

Books with a Story Line

The first tool to use is a bookmark to keep your place while you are reading. It has important questions that you should be asking yourself as you read each chapter.

HOW TO BE AN ACTIVE READER

WHILE I AM READING:

ASK QUESTIONS

- Who are the characters?
- What are they doing?
- What is the problem?
- Who is telling the story?

MAKE PREDICTIONS

- What is going to happen next?
- Why do I think this?

CONNECT TO THE TEXT

- Has anything like this happened to me?
- Does the book remind me of other books?
- Can I relate to any of the characters?

LEARN NEW VOCABULARY

- Are there any new words on this page?
- Have I seen this word before?
- Can I figure out what it means using the context?
- Do I need to look it up?

SUMMARIZE

- What happened in this chapter?
- Can I tell about the chapter in **one** sentence?

www.kandmcenter.com
Copyright ©2011 The K&M Center, Inc.

CHARACTER LIST

Use this to help you keep track of characters as you are reading.

CHARACTER'S NAME	DESCRIPTION	WHY ARE THEY IMPORTANT IN THE STORY?

CHAPTER SUMMARIES

Use this to jot down several important events in a chapter.

This way, if you have to write a summary, it is much easier to remember the big events in the book. Use as many copies of this page as you need, until you've completed one for each chapter.

CHAPTER _____:

CHAPTER _____:

CHAPTER _____:

CHAPTER _____:

CHAPTER _____:

CHAPTER _____:

Made in the USA
San Bernardino, CA
22 October 2017